Vegetation and environment in
Nydam, Denmark, during the Iron Age

Jernalderen i Nordeuropa

Vegetation and environment in Nydam, Denmark, during the Iron Age

Else Kolstrup

Sammenfatning på dansk

Carlsbergfondet, Nationalmuseet
& Moesgård Museum

Jysk Arkæologisk Selskab

Vegetation and environment in Nydam, Denmark, during the Iron Age

© Else Kolstrup and Jysk Arkæologisk Selskab 2009

Editor: Jørgen Ilkjær
Lay-out and cover: Ea Rasmussen
Proofreading: Anne Lise Hansen and Jørgen Ilkjær
Rentegning og grafisk bearbejdning: Ea Rasmussen

Press: Narayana Press, Gylling
Type: Palatino Linotype
Paper: Hello Silk
Binding: Damms Bogbinderi, Randers

Jysk Arkæologisk Selskabs Skrifter 65

ISBN: 978-87-88415-55-1
ISSN: 0107-2854

Publisher:
Jysk Arkæologisk Selskab
Moesgård
DK-8270 Højbjerg

Distribution:
Aarhus University Press
Langelandsgade 177
DK-8200 Århus N

Published by Carlsbergfondet, Nationalmuseet and Moesgård Museum
as a part of the project Jernalderen i Nordeuropa.

Steering group
Claus v. Carnap-Bornheim, Schloss Gottorf
Jan Skamby Madsen, Moesgård Museum
Per Kristian Madsen (chairman), Nationalmuseet

Table of contents

Foreword

In connection to the archeological research of the warfare sacrifices in Illerup, Ejsbøl and Nydam, a comprehensive amount of pollen samples has been collected; that is both in connection to the artefacts found and in pollen series in the different bog layers. The collection of pollen has several objectives. First and foremost it is possible to describe the vegetational development which contributes to the determination of the geneses of the specific bog. Secondly, the archeological find layers can be matched with the pollen series to achieve a relative dating.

After the excavations, work demanding analyses have been carried out in the laboratories. However, it is not until now with Else Kolstrup's publication of the pollen research from Nydam, a connection between the vegetational development and the warfare sacrifices has been established. Added to this is the description of the vegetation in the surrounding areas. The varied intensity of farming and the relation between land and forest are described in the research.

The scientific research is a significant supplement to the archeological observations, thus, it is important that the results are published as quickly as possible. In this way the results can be added to the analyses of the pollen series from the other bog finds and for this reason we have chosen this separate type of publication.

Jørgen Ilkjær

1. Abstract

Two sediment series have been collected in Nydam Bog, southern Jutland, Denmark, in close relation to archaeological finds. The series have been analysed for their pollen content and represent a vegetational development in the area during the younger part of the Iron Age for the time before, during and after deposition of large amounts of weapons and other artefacts in the bog. Before the deposition of the artefacts there seems to have been a well-established, stable situation with cultivation of various cereals and other crops and probably also husbandry and with added resources represented by a diverse natural vegetation. At the time of deposition of artefacts this situation changed to become more unstable and the agricultural pattern seems to have changed to a less intensive system or may possibly even have collapsed. More intensive cultivation re-occurred briefly a few decades later, but the human activity in the area does not seem to have returned to the original level after the time the archaeological objects were deposited. The two pollen series show that sampling close to archaeological finds imposes a possibility of disturbance of the sediments; but on the other hand it can make it possible to establish direct links between archaeological finds and vegetational and environmental changes within the same area.

2. Dansk resumé

Nydam mose i Sønderjylland er velkendt for sine mange Jernalderfund. Det gælder såvel de klassiske bådfund som mange fund af våben og andre genstande, der kom for dagen under Nationalmuseets udgravninger i 1990'erne. For at få information om den naturlige udvikling og den menneskelige aktivitet i dette rige fundområde, var det naturligt at også forsøge at rekonstruere jernalderens vegetationsudvikling ved hjælp af pollenanalytiske undersøgelser.

Denne artikel giver en oversigt over vegetationshistorien, som den kan rekonstrueres ud fra pollen analyser af to sedimentserier, Nydam profil 1 og 2, der blev udtaget i nær relation til de arkæologiske fund i den centrale del af Nydam Mose.

Pollendiagrammerne i figurerne 4 og 5 giver fra venstre information om sedimenterne og kulstof-14 dateringer. Dybder er angivet før selve diagrammerne, som indeholder forholdet mellem træ (AP) og ikke-træ (NAP) pollen efterfulgt af kurver for forskellige træer og buske. Derefter følger kurver for diverse urtepollen og andre genkendelige mikrofossiler. I diagrammerne er de nederste (ældste) lag underst og de yngste øverst, og hver vandret linie repræsenterer indholdet i en pollenprøve.

Pollenanalyserne viser, at der i bunden af mosen var meget gammel skovtørv; men derefter er der en brat overgang i sedimenterne til den yngre del af jernalderen. Det betyder, at der mangler sedimenter fra flere tusinde år, og ud fra pollenundersøgelsen er det nærliggende at antage, at der har været gravet tørv i Nydam Mose i tiden omkring eller kort tid efter Kristi fødsel.

De to pollendiagrammer repræsenterer vegetationsudviklingen i tiden for den yngre del af jernalderen, dvs. tiden før, under og efter den tid de mange genstande blev efterladt i mosen. Eftersom et tidsrum på nogle få hundrede år er repræsenteret ved mere end én meter sediment, giver det en høj opløselighed i pollendiagrammerne, så selv relativt hurtige ændringer kan detekteres i serierne. Eftersom der er undersøgt prøver med 2 cm mellemrum i en del af profilet Nydam 1, er det derfor muligt, at selv korte tidsrum på mindre end 5 år kan være repræsenteret i den del af serien.

De sedimenter, som blev aflejret før artefakterne blev efterladt, indeholder pollen, som peger på en vegetation, der repræsenterer et stabilt, veletableret system med dyrkning af forskellige slags korn og urter/grønsager, og der var sandsynligvis også dyrehold. Desuden var der højst sandsynligt kendskab til og brug af en diversitet af andre naturlige ressourcer.

Pollenindholdet i lagene, som rummer de arkæologiske fund, viser en ændring i vegetationen, som tyder på, at dyrkning og husdyrhold blev mindre intensive og dermed at forholdene i området blev mere ustabile; og det er endda muligt, at det daværende kultursystem stort set kollapsede.

Nogle få årtier senere var der en relativt svag genopblussen af det gamle landbrugssystem, men denne ser ud til kun at have været kortvarig, og pollenundersøgelserne peger på, at jernalderens tidligere niveau ikke blev genetableret i Nydam-området efter den tid, artefakterne var blevet efterladt i mosen.

Pollenindholdet i de to profiler, som er udtaget ca. 25 m fra hinanden, viser samme udvikling og sammensætning af plantevæksten i de højere områder omkring mosen; men de to diagrammer viser samtidigt, at udviklingen af vandplanterne på de to lokaliteter var forskellig gennem tiden, så det er muligt, at de to profiler kan repræsentere helt lokale forhold.

De to profiler, som er repræsenteret i diagrammerne, er valgt i direkte forbindelse med arkæologiske fund. Det betyder, at sedimenterne kan være oprodede, fordi jernalderens mennesker gik rundt i mosen, hvilket er en klar ulempe, hvis man ønsker en sedimentserie med en uforstyrret pollensedimentation. På den anden side giver den nære kontakt til arkæologien den store fordel, at der kan etableres en direkte årsag-virkning sammenhæng mellem menneskelig aktivitet og vegetationsudvikling.

For at fremme læseligheden i den efterfølgende engelske tekst er danske plantenavne nogle steder indføjet i teksten efter de latinske navne. Desuden er der givet en engelsk og en dansk oversættelse af de latinske navne i Appendix 1A i relation til deres placering i pollendiagrammerne, og i Appendix 1B er de latinske navne givet i alfabetisk orden efterfulgt af de engelske og danske.

3. Introduction

The Iron Age is well known in Denmark from several major archaeological excavations. Numerous artefacts elucidate various aspects of daily life as well as of more rare events and often the latter aspects have received relatively much attention. Nydam Bog (Fig. 1) with its exquisite boats, numerous weapons and other remarkable finds (e.g., Rieck et al. 1999) is a clear example of this. But during the Iron Age, as well as now, the daily chores and sustenance must have been in the focus during most of peoples' lives. Therefore, for a holistic reconstruction, it is necessary that investigations also include the natural conditions for daily life as they can be elucidated by geological and palaeobotanical investigations in and around the settlement area.

In Denmark there are several Holocene pollen records that cover the time of the Iron Age culture and from which the vegetational and environmental developments within various areas can be reconstructed. But so far the records have suffered from the drawback that they are from bogs and lakes at some distance from the archaeological finds so that a firm correlation between archaeological finds, and natural environmental developments are difficult to establish. The pollen records from Nydam represent the first case in Denmark from which Iron Age archaeological and natural environmental development can be directly related.

In 1991 two 1.5 m long sample series of peat were collected from open profiles in two localities in Nydam Bog (Fig. 2 and 3), and between 1991 and 1993 they were analysed for their contents of pollen and spores. During the very first counting it became clear that there was a gap of several thousand years in the sediment series. Owing to this c. 6000 years long gap there are no sediments from the time that represents most of the Mesolithic, all of the Neolithic, the Bronze Age and the early part of the Iron Age. Instead the two sampled series cover the time from around 100 AD and a few hundred years on, i.e., the younger part of the Iron Age. The deposition of the 1.5 m of sediment in Nydam Bog thus represents a high sedimentation rate with a time resolution of a decadal and even shorter time scale. The pollen series therefore give a possibility to detect changes in the bog and its surroundings of direct relevance to the archaeological finds.

In the following a brief overview of the geological setting of the area is presented and descriptions are given of the two profiles from which the pollen series are collected. This is followed by a general perusal of the use and limitations of pollen analysis before the pollen diagrams are described and interpreted for an outline of the Iron Age vegetational and environmental developments in and around Nydam Bog. Appendix 1A and 1B give translations of latin plant names.

4. Geological setting

The pollen diagrams and the archaeological finds in Nydam Bog (Nydam Mose) are located within the upstream part of a less than ½ km wide and about 5-6 km long northwest-southeast oriented valley that extends into Als Sund to the southeast (Fig. 1). At the present the locality of Nydam Bog forms a low lying, rather flat boggy pasture area surrounded by higher, dry land. The sediments in the bog consist of peat and gyttja and the subsoil in the surrounding higher areas is dominated by clayey till deposited by the Scandinavian ice (Jessen 1945). Locally, at some distance there are smaller areas with more sandy sediments (Jessen 1945). The surrounding area can therefore be regarded as fertile and rather diverse, thus giving possibility for good growing conditions for many different plants. Besides, the locality is only a few km from the open, yet relatively sheltered salt-brackish water of Als Sund in the western part of the Baltic Sea. A more comprehensive description of the basin and its sediment sequences is given in Andreasen & Christensen (1998), Christensen & Kolstrup (1998) and Jørgensen et al. (1998).

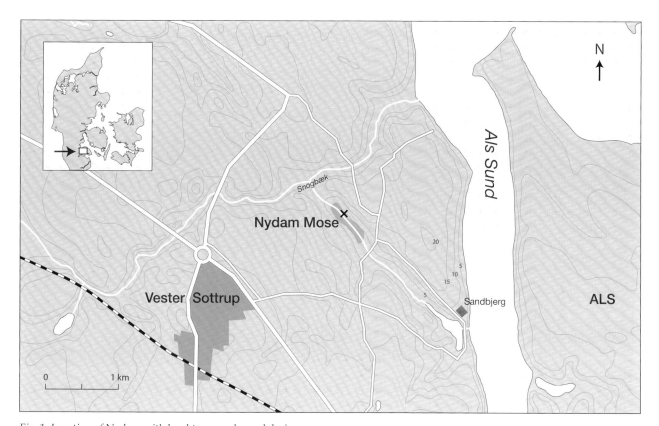

Fig. 1. Location of Nydam with local topography and drainage.

5. Field and laboratory methods

During the summer of 1991 samples for pollen analysis were collected from two open profiles, which were described in the field and later checked in the laboratory. In both profiles continuous 1.5 m long sample series were collected using three consecutive aluminium samplers, each half a metre long and 4 x 4 cm wide and deep (Fig. 2 and 3). The two series were situated c. 25 m apart. In the field, Nydam profile 1 was described jointly with Dr. C. Christensen, National Museum of Denmark. Also samples for ra-

Fig. 2. The sediments at the Nydam 1 series. The three vertical, 50 cm long, sample boxes include the layered gyttja and peat sediments of the locality. The 3 m level is found just above the lower arrow on the upper box.

Fig. 3. The sediments at the Nydam 2 series. The three vertical, 50 cm long, sample boxes include the layered gyttja and peat sediments of the locality. The horizontal line shows the 3 m level. The lower and upper shield layers cross the lower half of the middle sample box. There is a concentration of swords (not visible) in the dark right hand corner of the photo.

diocarbon dating from this profile were collected jointly with him and were chosen so that they could be related to the pollen profile and the archaeological finds. Nydam profile 2, which was located southeast of profile 1, was collected and described under time pressure from an open vertical exposure with two shield layers (Fig. 3 central, right hand part) and a concentration with several swords nearby.

In the laboratory the samples were further described and ½ cm³ sub-samples for pollen analysis were collected at intervals from the aluminium samplers. From series 1 the samples were collected in two turns. The first samples were taken between 4 and 13 cm apart. Following microscopic analysis of the first series additional, intervening samples were selected at interesting levels, so that, in parts of the final pollen profile, the distance between samples is only 2 cm.

Peat and gyttja contain not only pollen but also macroscopic plant remains and other sedimentary components. Therefore peat and gyttja samples need to go through a laboratory preparation procedure that removes unwanted material and leaves a concentration of pollen for the microscopical work:

In series 1 four tablets, each with 12.100 *Lycopodium clavatum* (*ulvefod in Danish)* spores (purchased from the Department of Quaternary Geology, University of Lund, Sweden) were added to each ½ cm³ sample for calculation of the pollen concentrations (cf. Stockmarr 1971). The samples from this series were also sieved through 10 μm gauze to eliminate small organic particles that could disturb the view of the pollen (Kolstrup 2005). In series 2 no *Lycopodium* tablets were added, neither were these samples sieved in 10 μm gauze. All samples were treated with 10% HCl to remove lime (chalk) followed by boiling in 10% KOH to eliminate humic acid. Subsequently the samples were sieved in 224 μm gauze to remove coarse organic particles before they underwent Erdtman acetolysis to remove cellulose (e.g. Moore et al. 1991). Sandy samples were treated with $ZnBr_2$ with a specific gravity of 2 to remove the minerogenic particles and by now the remaining organic material had become highly concentrated in pollen. The samples were washed in 10% KOH to make them basic before they were embedded in glycerol and stained with basic fuchsine. Finally an appropriate amount

Fig. 4. Percentage diagram from Profile Nydam 1. To the left are sediment descriptions followed by radiocarbon ages of dated layers. The number of terrestrial pollen in the sum for each sample is followed by a depth scale. Each horizontal line represents a sample and the vertical curves show the changes through time graphically. In the main diagram to the left AP (arboreal pollen) indicates pollen from trees and NAP (non-arboreal pollen) includes pollen from other terrestrial plants including spore plants. Individual curves for the various tree pollen are shown first followed by pollen from terrestrial herbs in alphabetic order of families followed by terrestrial Pteridophytes (karsporeplanter), water plants and other information. In the diagram some types have t. after their names. This indicates that there are more pollen type in the group, but they can not be distinguished. The percentage scales for the black and white curves respectively is given to the left below the diagram. Translation of many of the Latin names is given in Appendix 1A and 1B. For further information see text.

Fig. 5. Percentage diagram from Profile Nydam 2. To the left are sediment descriptions followed by the number of terrestrial pollen in the sum for each sample, which in turn is followed by a depth scale. Each horizontal line represents a sample and the vertical curves show the changes through time graphically. In the main diagram to the left AP (arboreal pollen) indicates pollen from trees and NAP (non-arboreal pollen) includes pollen from other terrestrial plants including spore plants. Individual curves for the various tree pollen are shown first followed by pollen from terrestrial herbs in alphabetic order of families followed by terrestrial Pteridophytes, water plants and other information. In the diagram some types have t. after their names. This indicates that there are more pollen type in the group, but they can not be palynologically distinguished. The percentage scales for the black and white curves respectively is given to the left below the diagram. For further information see text.

Fig. 4 and 5 are separate appendices and can be found in the back of the publication.

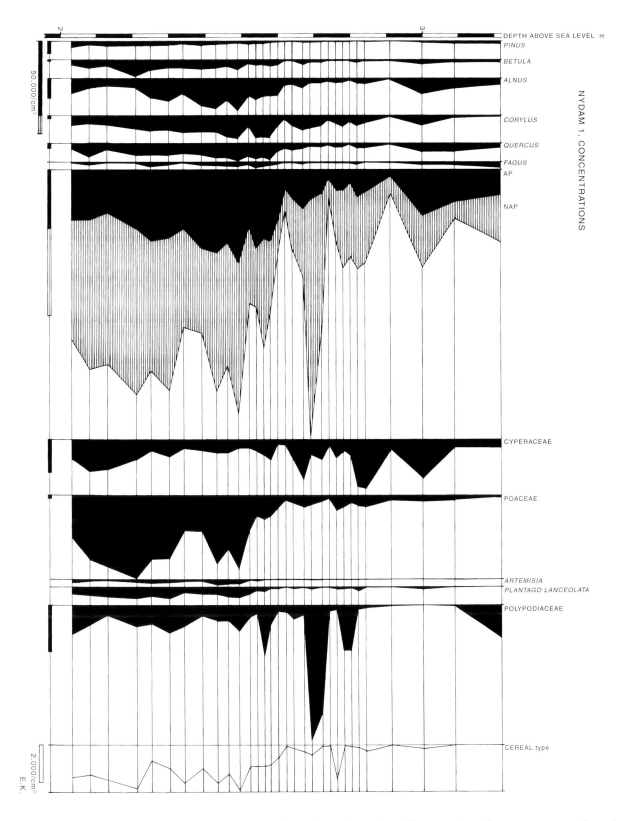

Fig. 6. Pollen concentrations of selected pollen types. The values indicate the number of the respective pollen types or groups for each cm³ of sample as calculated on the basis of the added Lycopodium (ulvefod) spores.

19

of residue was transferred to an object glass, covered by a thin cover-slip and the object glass was marked for identification before the microscopic analysis.

In most samples a sum of 500 or more palynomorphs (pollen and spores) from terrestrial plants (arboreal (tree) pollen (AP) + non-arboreal pollen (NAP)) was counted. In each sample the percentages of individual pollen types are calculated based on this sum and the results are presented graphically in the enclosed percentage diagrams of Fig. 4 (locality Nydam 1) and 5 (locality Nydam 2) (see further below). For locality Nydam 1 the total number of selected pollen types in each cm^3 of sediment was calculated on the basis of the amount of added *Lycopodium* spores. The result is given in a concentration diagram (Fig. 6).

6. Description of the profiles

6.1. Profile Nydam 1 (Fig. 2)

The profile is described from top to bottom. In the whole of the profile there were fresh, vertical *Equisetum* (padderokke) roots.

3.59 - 3.30 m: Disturbed top soil.
   The upper limit of the sample boxes for pollen analyses was at 3.22 m. A sample for radiocarbon dating (K 6054) was collected between 3.04 and 3.07 m.
3.30 - 2.87 m: Indistinctly layered, brown, fibrous, generally only slightly humified peat with many mosses in some horizons. At 3.25 m was a seed of *Potamogeton* (vandaks).
2.87 - 2.75 m: This sediment is similar to the overlying part except that it is less fibrous. Laterally a single carr hummock was present.
2.75 - 2.66 m: Carr peat with a low content of gyttja or possibly decomposed peat. Single macrofossils of *?Dryopteris* (mangeløv), *Equisetum* rhizomes.
2.66 - 2.60 m: Dark olive brown, slightly greenish, fibrous peat and mosses with some gyttja. This is an archaeological find layer, laterally with horizontally laying sticks, 2-3 cm in diameter, with pointshaped ends as well as other artefacts. Radiocarbon sample K 5808 is from a pointed stick in this layer.
2.60 - 2.45 m: Gyttja with coarser material. From bottom to top there is a gradual transition from a gyttja:peat proportion of c. 3:1 to c. 1:1 owing to an increase in coarse fibrous matter and mosses. In the middle part of this unit there are seeds of *Nymphaea alba* (hvid åkande). Opercula of *Bithynia tentaculata* (sumpsnegl) are abundant in the lower part.

2.45 - 2.31 m: Light olive grey gyttja rich in lime, locally with lime concentrations, mainly along layering. The sediment is layered and has a very low content of fibrous material.
2.31 - 2.26 m: Like the above, but darker grey-olive to brown and with less lime. There is presence of fist sized stones.
2.26 - 2.18 m: Rather similar to the above, but darker brown-slightly reddish, stratified gyttja with a little lime and sand. Presence of pieces of *Anodonta* (dammusling) shells and imprints of Nymphaceae (åkande) rhizomes.
2.18 - 1.98 m: Light grey-olive lime-containing detritus gyttja. It contains a low content of fibrous matter and fragments of plant stems and, in the lower part, single *Bithynia* opercula.
1.98 m and beneath: Abrupt transition to dark brown, strongly decomposed, relatively dry and compact peat with pieces of wood and a few fine roots. The lower limit of the sample boxes for pollen analyses in Fig. 2 is at 1.86 m. *Alnus* (el) roots for radiocarbon dating (sample K 5809) were extracted from between 1.98 and 1.93 m.

6.2. Profile Nydam 2 (Fig. 3).

Also in this profile there were fresh *Equisetum* roots throughout.

3.24 - 3.16 m: Dark brown, humified, probably reworked, fibrous peat.
3.16 - 3.06 m: Brown, very fibrous and rather coarse moss peat with stem fragments.

3.06 - 2.92 m: Brown to light brown fibrous peat. Slightly more fibrous than the underlying part.

2.92 - 2.84 m: Like the underlying part, but lighter in colour and less fibrous.

2.84 - 2.73 m: Brown to light brown, horizontally layered, very fibrous moss peat like the underlying, but it is coarser and contains small peaces of twigs. This is the most fibrous part of the section.

2.73 - 2.55 m: Brown, fibrous peat with mosses and stem fragments as well as roots.

2.55 - 2.45 m: Brown, indistinctly layered, fibrous moss peat with fine roots. Coarser than in the layer between 2.31 and 2.43 m.

2.45 - 2.43 m: Upper shield.

2.43 - 2.31 m: Brown to dark brown fibrous peat with gyttja. There are mosses and plant fragments, and the sediment is relatively more rich in fibrous matter in the upper part.

2.31 - 2.29 m: Lower shield.

2.29 - 2.10 m: Brown to dark brown detritus gyttja with peat and an increasing amount of mosses upward. Slightly more compact than below.

2.10 - 1.92 m: Transitional part with the colour becoming darker upwards and a low content of sand, lime and *Bithynia* opercula.

1.92 - 1.74 m: Olive brown to slightly grey, layered, lime rich, elastic gyttja with some mosses. Single *Bithynia* opercula are present the lower part. Some layers are sandy, especially around 1.85 m.

Investigation of deeper layers was prevented by water.

7. Pollen analysis: principles, applications and limitations

Pollen are the male, fertilizing cells from flower plants. In size most pollen are in the order of 20 to 40 µm (0,02-0,04 mm), but some are much larger, for example spruce (*Picea* (gran)) pollen can be 100 µm and others, such as some *Primula* (kodriver) pollen are only around 10 µm. Such sizes mean that pollen can only be identified through a microscope.

Pollen (and spores) consist of an inner, softer part protected by a harder shell of so-called sporopollenin. If pollen and spores land in a bog or lake with non-oxidizing moist to wet conditions the sporopollenin shell can become preserved for thousands of years. If, on the other hand, the pollen is exposed to oxygen the shell becomes corroded, and especially thin walled pollen may disappear. Sediments that have been oxidized may consequently give false pictures of the past vegetations with overrepresentation of thick walled and/or easily recognisable pollen types. But under good preservation conditions new layers can become deposited during succeeding years and the sediments thus build up a vegetation-history book told by the successive layers of pollen that landed through time in the bog or lake and became fossilized there.

Each plant species has its own pollen type with specific morphological characteristics, and as a rule of thumb the closer the plant species are related the more similar their pollen are. As a consequence pollen from different species within a family can usually not be distinguished from each other during microscopic analysis. For example pollen from the large grass family can not normally be separated; however, some cultivated species have relatively large pollen with specific characteristics so that well preserved pollen from the cultivated grasses wheat (*Triticum*) (including einkorn and emmer), rye (*Secale cereale*) and tentatively also from barley (*Hordeum*) can be reasonably safely determined in a good microscope with phase- and/or interference contrast and at least 1000 times magnification. Reliable determinations also require good reference samples and literature with high-standard determination keys. In the present investigation a pollen and spore reference collection of *c.* 1000 slides was used in addition to a number of determination keys (Fægri & Iversen 1966; Moore et al. 1991; the series by Punt as the main editor "The Northwest European Pollen Flora" Volumes 1-6 from between 1976 and 1988; as well as some other, more specialized works).

Different plant species produce different amounts of pollen and spread them in different ways. Some plants, like wheat, are self pollinating and produce few pollen that only need to travel a short distance. Others are dependant on insects, bees for example, for their spreading and in this case more pollen is produced. Pollen from plants with self- or insect pollination are normally very few in fossil records from bogs and lakes both because there are relatively few pollen and because their spreading range is limited. In contrast, pollen from wind pollinated species are often abundant. This is because wind pollinated plants, rye is an example here, produce huge amounts of pollen, a necessity if a pollen grain must have a chance to land on the style, the receptive female part, of the same species. Wind borne pollen grains can be transported over many hundred kilometres and it is this group that normally makes up the main part of pollen in the fossil samples. It follows that wind pollinated plants become relatively over-represented in the samples, and besides, pollen from plants that did not grow in the vicinity can also be represented. In relation to an interpretation of pollen diagrams it therefore needs to be remembered that just a single or very few pollen grains of a self- or insect pollinating species, flax (*Linum*) for example, can represent a cultivated field with this species in the surroundings. In turn a few pollen from a wind pollinating plant such as rye need not have come from the immediate vicinity.

It is well known that also in the past some plants, such as cereals, were cultivated, and that others were favoured by presence of grazing animals and various human activities. In a classical overview paper by Behre (1981) a general outline of this knowledge is summarised as a "rule-of-thumb" classification scheme of various pollen taxa according to their indications of anthropogenic influence. From this overview the pollen of *Triticum* (hvedetyper) and *Secale* (rug) for example are indicators of cultivation, while others such as for example *Plantago lanceolata*, *P. major* (vejbredarter) and *Rumex* (skræppe) are often regarded as indicators of other human activities and are thus taken as anthropogenic indicators once they are present in fair numbers.

Most investigations that try to combine evidence from archaeological investigations on the one hand and geological/geobotanical investigations on the other face the difficulty of disjunct localities. In most cases the archaeological evidence is found on dry land and the botanical part at some distance in wet/moist localities where the taphonomical conditions were favourable for preservation of organic matter. In such situations, therefore, it can be difficult to link the two sets of data sufficiently accurately.

The Nydam Bog investigation has the advantage that there is a direct connection between the sampled sediments which accumulated in the bog over the years and the archaeological finds. This is a rare coincidence which, at least in theory, makes it possible to detect possible causes and effects between vegetational development and human activity. At the same time it gives problems as illustrated by the dissimilarities in the composition and succession of water and reed pollen in the two diagrams (see also the chapter "Profile Nydam 2, percentage diagram and comparison to Nydam 1" below) because trampling, digging and other activities can have, and in section 2 almost certainly has, caused mixing of the sediments so that pollen from different years can have become mixed or the layers turned upside down. Likewise, other activities like swimming or eel fishing as well as bringing large and heavy boats into the area can be expected to have affected the sediments. Clearly, such possibilities of disturbance renders it more difficult to make reliable reconstructions of past local environmental developments from the diagrams.

8. The pollen diagrams

8.1. Structure

In the pollen diagrams (Fig. 4 and 5 Enclosures) the individual samples are placed in vertical succession. The level of each sample is indicated (in m above sea level) to the left together with the number of pollen included in the sum, the general sediment descriptions and, where relevant, the radiocarbon ages. To facilitate the reading consecutive percentage values for each taxon are connected into pollen curves. This has as a consequence that information which could have been gained from the pollen in between is left out; so during the reading it needs to be remembered that the intervening sediments might have revealed additional, but unrecorded information.

Figures 4 and 5 are percentage diagrams from profile Nydam 1 and 2 respectively and Figure 6 shows tentative, absolute values of selected taxa in profile Nydam 1, i.e., the number within the selected pollen groups or types that were deposited in each cm³ of sediment.

In the pollen diagrams and the text below the names of the plants are given in Latin following an international scientific tradition. To facilitate the reading Appendix 1A and 1B give the Latin names of some of the taxa together with the corresponding plant names in English and Danish.

The percentages of various pollen types that were identified during the counting are shown along the horizontal lines in figures 4 and 5. In the main AP-NAP (arboreal pollen – nonarboreal pollen) diagrams to the left the mutual percentages of tree pollen and non-tree pollen are given for a general impression of the forest – open land relationship during time. This is followed by percentages of the various tree and shrub pollen taxa. Then come pollen from terrestrial herbs organized alphabetically according to their latin family names followed by spores from terrestrial Pteridophytes (ferns). In turn this is followed by pollen and spores from water plants, non-determinable (usually damaged) pollen and spores, microscopically identifiable plant fragments, and finally *Sphagnum* spores, algae and more than 10 µm long charcoal particles. To the far right in diagram Nydam 1 the percentages of the added *Lycopodium* spores (based on the same sum as the other curves) are given for a general assessment of the pollen content in the samples, i.e., higher *Lycopodium* percentages indicate lower pollen content.

In the diagrams many taxa are represented by both a black and a white curve. The black curves give the percentages as indicated in the scale bar in the lower left, while the white (open) curves represent the same values multiplied by 10 to better indicate low percentages.

In the diagrams the pollen types are not clustered according to ecological requirements or anthropogenic relevance as it is sometimes seen in pollen diagrams related to archaeological investigations. This is because 1) only few pollen can be determined to species level as mentioned above and, therefore, some pollen curves (taxa) can include pollen both from plant species that were cultivated or used by people and from others without indicator value. And 2) there is a possibility that many plants, which are today regarded as weeds or of no particular use could have been used in the past. By classifying them according to present-day knowledge and uses could introduce a rigidity with the interpretation that may not be justified.

8.2. Outline of the contents of the diagrams

This subchapter gives a descriptive overview of the contents of the pollen diagram. In the succeeding chapter it is attempted to date the pollen phases, and finally an outline is given of how the vegetation development and the human activity could have been in Nydam through time in chapter 10.

8.2.1. Profile Nydam 1, percentage and concentration diagrams (Fig. 4 and 6)

Pollen diagram Profile Nydam 1 is divided into a lower sample at 1.97 m and the remaining part of the diagram between 2.03 m and 3.22 m.

At this stage of the perusal there is reason to draw the attention to the *Lycopodium* percentage curve to the right in digram Profile Nydam 1 and to the concentration diagram from the same series in figure 6. As noted above lower *Lycopodium* percentages in the percentage diagram indicate higher pollen concentration values in a sample possibly because of slower sedimentation, and vice versa. In the diagrams it can be seen that the pollen concentration values are fairly constant between 2.03 m and 2.58 m. The level at 2.60 m marks the transition to the archaeological find layer. From around this level the *Lycopodium* values fluctuate strongly, sometimes reaching very high percentages, and thus low pollen concentrations (Figures 4 and 6). Especially the tree pollen content from c. 2.60 m and up has decreased (as shown by lower AP values in the concentration diagram). Such changes suggest more unstable sedimentary conditions and/or generally reduced pollen content, with a reduced influx of tree pollen being relatively more pronounced.

The lower sample (at 1.97m) has much *Tilia* (lind) and some *Alnus*, *Corylus*, *Pinus* and *Quercus* (el, hassel, fyr og eg), but there is no *Fraxinus*, *Carpinus*, *Fagus* (ask, avnbøg, bøg) or culture indicators. From a comparison with published Danish and north German pollen records (e.g. Andersen 1954; Dörfler, 1989; Behre & Kučan 1994; Odgaard 1994) this indicates an early Atlantic age.

The part between 2.03 m and 3.22 m shows a variety of forest taxa, notably of *Quercus*, *Corylus*, *Alnus*

and *Betula*. Also *Fagus* is present and reaches somewhat higher percentages in the upper part while *Ulmus*, *Fraxinus* and *Carpinus* have low values. Many tree pollen curves have relatively low values in the lower part up to 2.21 m and between 2.67 m and 2.91 m. There are low percentages of *Tilia*, a tree which has low production and poor spreading of pollen as it is also the case with many of the representatives of the Rosaceae family. *Taxus* (taks), which hardly grows wild in Denmark today, is sporadically present.

There is a high variety of terrestrial herb pollen throughout, and already from the start at 2.03 m there is fairly good representation of *Plantago lanceolata*, *Rumex* and *Urtica* (nælde) as well as of *Calluna* (lyng). Poaceae are particularly abundant in the lower part and include pollen from the cereals *Triticum* type, *Hordeum* type and *Secale*. At 2.60 m, the find layer, and upward the cereal pollen decreases both in terms of percentage and concentration values, and also *Plantago major*, Chenopodiaceae (salturtfamilien), *Cannabis/Humulus* (hamp/humle) and *Pteridium* (ørnebregne) decrease from around this level. In the diagram there is continuous representation of Cyperaceae and Filicales which both increase from around 2.60 m up to 2.84 m.

In a single sample at 2.76 m within this part there is relatively good representation of the various cereal pollen types as well as of Poaceae, in addition to single pollen finds of *Linum* (possibly the cultivated type) and *Prunella* (brunelle) type. Above 2.76 m culture indicators are again more sporadically represented. In the upper two samples (3.09 m and 3.22 m) the sediments had probably been exposed to oxygen because many pollen and spores (indet. pollen + spores to the right in the diagram) were too damaged for reliable identification.

The fairly diverse lake and reed vegetation is represented by the curves in the right hand part of the diagram, but it is possible that also a few other pollen taxa such as f.x. *Bidens* (brøndsel) type, Juncaceae (siv), and *Caltha* type (kabbeleje) should be seen within the context of the lake and reed vegetation. In the lowermost part there is much *Potamogeton/Triglochin* (vandaks/trehage) together with *Nymphaea* (åkande) and *Sparganium* (pindsvineknop) so there must have been open water at the site. From around 2.21 m this is followed by water lilies, *Sparganium* and *Potamogeton*, which in turn are followed by other water plants and there are single *Ruppia* (havgræs) pollen and hair from *Ceratophyllum* (hornblad). Also around and after the archaeological find layer there is a variety of water and reed plants including *Lemna*, *Sparganium* and *Typha latifolia* (andemad, pindsvineknop, dunhammer) and others, and in the upper part there is *Scheuchzeria*, *Menyanthes*, *Pedicularis*, *Typha latifolia* (blomstersiv, bukkeblad, troldurt, dunhammer) and single *Eu-Potamogeton* (vandaks).

8.2.2. Profile Nydam 2, percentage diagram (Fig. 5) and comparison to profile Nydam 1

Diagram Nydam 2 (Fig. 5) represents a section of peat and gyttja that was collected in close connection with a major accumulation of weapons and other archaeological finds. In Nydam 2 there are longer distances between consecutive samples than in Nydam 1.

With regard to the tree pollen percentages and the representation of anthropogenic indicators there is general agreement between the records Nydam 1 and 2 even if, for example, *Fagus* has comparatively lower percentages between 2,41 m and 2,71 m in Nydam 2. As it is the case in Nydam 1 there is also a decrease in pollen from cereals and grasses at the level of the lower find layer, which in Nydam 2 coincides with the lower shield layer; and also in this diagram there is some decrease of the anthropogenic indicators *Plantago lanceolata*, *Rumex* and *Urtica* and a rise in Filicales at or shortly above this level in the diagram. Overall, taking into account the different sample distances in the two diagrams, which may blur the overview, there are many general parallels in the trends of the curves of pollen deriving from terrestrial taxa. It is therefore proposed that the find layer in Nydam 1 and the lower shield layer in Nydam 2 are (almost) contemporaneous.

On the other hand a closer look at the trends of some water and reed pollen curves in the two records shows that there are a number of differences between them: *Nymphaea* pollen and the Nymphaceae hair co-

incide better in Nydam 2 than in 1. Further, in 2 the upper *Potamogeton* maximum coincides with a *Nymphaea* minimum while in 1 it coincides with a maximum. In Nydam 2 a *Sparganium* maximum coincides with a Filicales maximum, while in 1 the *Sparganium* top is relatively lower than the Filicales maximum. Further, in 2 there is presence of *Potamogeton* and *Nymphaea* pollen and Nymphaceae hair between 2.32 and 2.49 m, which is above the comparative level in 1. Clearly the two diagrams show different developments of the hydrophytes .

There may be at least three explanations for such differences: 1) there could have been two separate lakes each with individual, yet contemporaneous developments of the waterplants. This is not regarded as very likely because the two localities are so close together that there could easily have been spreading of species between them thus creating parallel vegetational developments; 2) they represent different times of development, i.e., the digging and filling of the holes could have been out of phase. This possibility is regarded as less likely because of the similarities in the trends of the curves of pollen from terrestrial taxa. Possibility 3) takes into account the location of the profiles in relation to the archaeological finds: in diagram 2 the close presence of artefacts indicates both digging and walking at or very close to the site and besides, the trends of the pollen curves of water plants in addition to the trend of, for example, the *Fagus* curve give reason to suspect reworking and mixing of sediments in locality 2. Diagram Nydam 1 is thought to be less disturbed because it shows more short-term changes of various pollen curves and a more straightforward succession of the vegetational development. The pollen concentration values are fairly constant in the lower part of the diagram, which might suggest a stable depositional environment up to the find layer. This, however, does not exclude a possibility of mixing of sediments in Nydam 1. For example there are stones, which are believed to have been thrown into the lake below the find layer, and their settling could have caused some vertical mixing as could unrecorded human activity in and around the lake.

At a higher level in the diagram (between 2.71 and 2.80 m) the *Fagus* curve has a relatively well marked increase in Nydam 2. This increase is less well marked at the corresponding level in Nydam 1. Other transitions, for example of *Quercus*, are also better marked in 2 than in 1 so that, thereby, gaps in the sediment record are hinted at above the find layer in Nydam 2, or, alternatively though less likely, there could have been vertical mixing of sediments in the upper part of Nydam 1.

9. Age of the series and resolution of the diagrams

It has previously been pointed out that there is a major gap in the sediment series in Nydam Bog as indicated by both the radiocarbon ages of the peat and the pollen records. The radiocarbon method can give a direct age of the deposits from which the samples have been collected provided uncontaminated material is used for the dating. Pollen analysis, on the other hand, is not a dating method in itself, but in some cases it can be used as an indirect dating method. This is the case when a pollen diagram represents a continuous sediment series that reflects a vegetational development with characteristic changes in the trends and mutual frequencies of individual plant taxa. Such changes can then be compared with similar, well dated developments elsewhere. By means of radiocarbon ages and estimated ages of correlatable horizons in the pollen diagrams, ages of intervening layers can be tentatively assessed, and subsequently sedimentation rates can be estimated and vegetation density and composition through time can be reconstructed.

9.1. Radiocarbon ages

Three radiocarbon ages are related to pollen profile Nydam 1. The deepest is from the basic peat between 1.98 and 1.93 m, one dates the archaeological find layer next to the diagram at that locality and the third gives an age of sediments c. 45 cm above the find layer.

The ages are all conventional datings done at the radiocarbon laboratory in Copenhagen and are calibrated according to Stuiver et al. (1998).

Before the dating proper, the carr peat was washed through a 1 mm sieve and roots and *Equisetum*-rhizomes were removed from the > 1mm fraction. Sub-

sequently the remaining humic matter was removed in the radiocarbon laboratory before the dating was carried out on the remaining organic matter.

Sample C7. K-6054. Carr peat. The sample was collected at 3,04-3,07 m just next to pollen series Nydam 1.Conventional age uncalibrated: 1610 ± 75 ^{14}C a BP (a = years). Calibrated with ± 1 standard deviation to: 380-540 a AD.

Sample C6. K-5808. Peaces from 2-3 cm thick pointed sticks with bark in the find layer. The sticks were located laterally between 0.5 m and 1.3 m east of pollen series Nydam 1 at levels 2,57 and 2,61 m. Conventional age uncalibrated: 1660 ± 75 ^{14}C a BP. Calibrated with ± 1 standard deviation: 260-530 a AD.

Sample C5. K-5809. Alder root wood, up to 3 cm thick, from the basic peat. The sample was collected at 1,97-2,07 m next to pollen series Nydam 1. Conventional age uncalibrated: 7020 ± 110 ^{14}C a BP. Calibrated with ± 1 standard deviation: 5990-5750 a BC.

9.2. Archaeological ages

Archaeological ages come from dendrochronological investigations and comparisons of artefacts of similar style elsewhere. According to Bonde and Daly (2000) only relatively few pieces of wood were suited for dendrochronological investigations. The results that are presented by these authors suggest deposition at different times between c. 200 AD and around or a few decades after 300 AD, but the lake may have grown over as late as 400 AD (Andreasen & Christensen 1998).

9.3. Ages deducted from the pollen diagram

The lower sample in diagram 1 contains *Tilia* (lind) and other elements from the mixed deciduous forest, but lacks *Fraxinus*, *Carpinus*, *Fagus* (ask, avnbøg, bøg) and culture indicators. A comparison with published records from Denmark (e.g., Mikkelsen 1949; Andersen 1954; Odgaard 1994), southern Sweden (Nilsson 1935; 1964; Gaillard 1984) and northern Germany (Dörfler 1989; Behre & Kučan 1994) shows that this sample is of early Atlantic age in accordance with the radiocarbon age of 7.020 ± 110 BP in this profile and 7.030 ± 115 BP elsewhere in the bog (Andreasen & Christensen 1998).

The sediment in the succeeding part is gyttja, and it was expected that a radiocarbon date would be in error (cf. Olsson 1985). Therefore, radiocarbon dating of this part was not attempted.

Between the samples at 1.97 m and 2.03 m there is a marked sedimentological and palynological shift to a vegetation that includes fair representation of *Fagus*, continuous presence of *Carpinus* and various cultivated species including rye (*Secale*). The tree pollen composition together with the culture indicators in this part and higher suggests that the start of deposition of this sediment started during the Subatlantic at the time of or after the introduction of *Secale* (rye) in the area. Sporadic finds of *Secale* are recorded from pre-Roman time in northern Germany and southern Scandinavia (e.g., Andersen 1954; Dörfler 1989; Behre 1992; Rasmussen 2005), and a more or less continuous rye pollen curve is found from c. 100 AD onward (e.g., Wiethold 1998). It is therefore suggested that the start of the Nydam pollen series 1 at the level of 2.03 m is from about or, more likely, after 100 AD. This means that the time gap between the samples at 1.97 m and 2.03 m is in the order of 6000 years.

In the upper samples *Fagus* has attained somewhat higher percentages, but they are still relatively low as compared to the late Subatlantic values in lake Bundsø (Andersen 1954), which is 8 km north of Nydam Bog. In accordance with the ^{14}C age from Nydam between 3,04 m and 3,07 m the pollen diagrams therefore also point to an age within the early Subatlantic, and consequently, except for the lower, Atlantic, sample at 1.97 m, the whole pollen series represents part of the Iron Age.

9.4. Sedimentation rates and resolution of the series

The ^{14}C ages and the sedimentary record in combination with the rather low, fluctuating pollen concentrations in the upper half of the concentration diagram from locality 1, suggest that this part of the profile was deposited within decades. If the ^{14}C dates are taken face value, 45 cm of sediment would have been deposited in say, between 50 and 80 years. It follows that, as a mean, each cm of sediment was deposited in less than 2 years. Considering the strongly fluctuating AP (tree pollen) and NAP (non-tree) pollen concentrations the deposition may have been faster in those parts where the pollen concentrations are lower and relatively slower where they are higher than the mean. With a sample analysed at every 2 cm as it is the case with the central part of Nydam 1, the time resolution between consecutive pollen samples for this part of the diagram may be in the order of 3-4 years, again as a mean, and quick environmental changes can therefore be expected to be recorded in the diagram for the time around and in particular after the deposition of the artefacts in the bog. For comparison 1,4 m of annually laminated sediments were deposited between 96 BC and 205 AD in Lake Belau near Neumünster, i.e., the sedimentation rate in that locality was one cm for each *c.* 2.2 years, but decreased after that time (Garbe-Schönberg et al. 1998; Wiethold 1998).

The high pollen concentration values in the series beneath the find layer show that the deposition rate was generally lower and more constant through time than in the upper part. For this lower part the sedimentation rate is more difficult to assess because the start at 2.03 m is not well dated; but most probably these c. 55 cm of sediment were deposited in less than 400 years, possibly only half of this, i.e. the mean sedimentation rate could have been in the order of at least one cm for each 8 years.

Overall, from the above it is probable that the c. 1.2 m of sediment between 2.03 m and 3.22 m in diagram 1 represents a development that lasted a few hundred years at the most.

10. Vegetation developments and human activity in Nydam

The lowermost sample in Nydam 1 represents the vegetation in the area before human influence became detectable in the pollen diagrams. In the higher, clayey areas around the bog at that time there was forest with relative abundance of lime (*Tilia* – insect pollinated), as well as other elements from the mixed deciduous forest such as oak (*Quercus*), elm (*Ulmus*) and hazel (*Corylus*). In moister parts, probably closer to the bog, alder (*Alnus*) seems to have been common. In the bog there were sedges (Cyperaceae) and possibly also some grasses (Poaceae) and ferns (Filicales), yet, the latter could also have formed understorey in moist, relatively open forest. The diversity of herbs was rather moderate and there seem to have been no water plants. The combination of organic sediment and the local vegetation points to relatively moist local conditions without open water in the depression at the time these pollen were deposited.

As already mentioned in the introduction, the pollen analysis immediately revealed that there was a hiatus of about 6000 years in the sediment record. Considering the sharp sedimentary transition in addition to the generally good preservation and the rather low amount of reworked pollen in the overlying samples the gap in the record probably has to be explained by human digging into older peat deposits. The reason why peat was dug can only be speculative: it could have been for fuel and/or constructional or other domestic purposes and/or the peat was removed to create an inland harbour. From the tree pollen curves it seems that there would have been sufficient wood for fuel in the surroundings so that there might not have been a pressing need for digging of peat for this purpose. Even if there was burning of wood in the Nydam area, the charcoal curve (to the right in the diagram) does not suggest excessive burning of wood for the time represented by the lower part of the diagram.

The pollen diagrams show that from the time the sediment at 2.03 m in Profile Nydam 1 was deposited and from the start of deposition in Nydam 2, there was open water in the area, at least in those parts of the bog where the two pollen sections were collected. This presence of open water could have been a result of peat digging, but other possibilities can not be exluded. Whether the explanation is a change in natural conditions or it is caused by human digging activities in the area, or both, the result was sufficiently deep, open water for growth of water plants; and with time new sediments accumulated.

10.1. The pre-findlayer time

During the time represented by the record between 2.03 cm and 2.58 m, i.e., up to the find layer in Nydam 1 and the part beneath the lower shield layer in Nydam 2 (the pre-findlayer time in the following), the forest around Nydam Bog contained a mixture of different trees including birch, oak, hazel and single elms, aspen and beeches (for the time correlation see further the chapter "The time around and after deposition of the find layer" below). Most of the trees probably grew on the fertile, clayey soils in the higher parts of the area around the bog, but there was also alder and some willows which may have occupied moister growing sites and possibly birches could have grown in the moister places too. From the mutual proportion between arboreal and non-arboreal pollen it may be suggested that the forest during this pre-findlayer time was rather open (compare e.g., Groenman-van Waateringe 1986). The vegetation in the lake points to open, neutral, mesotrophic water during this time.

During the pre-findlayer time there was a very diverse herbal flora. Grasses were common, but in particular there is presence of pollen from cultivated plants together with strong representation of plants that are often regarded as anthropogenic indicators, such as *Artemisia, Plantago lanceolata, Rumex, Filipendula, Urtica* (bynke, vejbred, skræppe, mjødurt, nælde) and many others that could either have been used or could have been favoured by human activities. The pollen diagrams thus clearly show that there was human activity around the lake with cultivated areas and various kinds of crops.

Cultivation of cereals included *Triticum* types and most probably also *Hordeum* and *Avena*, and possibly *Secale*.

In spite of the relatively few pollen of *Triticum* in the diagram this self-pollinating cereal type is found so regularly that it may nevertheless have been common. The *Triticum* pollen type includes various types of edible grains such as bread wheat, einkorn and emmer and possibly also spelt (dinkel) which are known from seed analysis in northern Germany and are thought to have been cultivated there from before year 0 AD (Behre 1990).

The same may have been the case with *Hordeum* which includes various types of barley. Unfortunately the pollen of this type includes not only barley but also certain wind pollinated wild grasses, which makes the determination uncertain; yet from findings in neighbouring areas, for example central southern Jutland (Henriksen 2003) and western Jutland (Robinson 2000) it seems almost certain that hulled barley was also cultivated in Nydam.

Rye, *Secale cereale*, is know from many Iron Age pollen diagrams in northern Europe and it is known to have been cultivated in southern Denmark around 400 AD (Henriksen 2003); and from that time and on rye is continuously present in a pollen curve from the island Funen. In that locality rye pollen is also present, discontinuously, during the preceeding time (Rasmussen 2005). In the Esbjerg area in western Jut-

land presence of seeds is documented from the Early Roman Iron Age (Robinson 2000). In the northeastern part of the Netherlands rye was, together with hulled barley, the most important crop plant between the first and fifth century AD (van Zeist & Palfenier-Vegter, 1991/1992). In pollen diagrams elsewhere for the time corresponding to the pre-findlayer in the Nydam diagrams rye has usually low percentages, and Behre (1992) leaves the question open if low percentages of this wind pollinated species in areas with rich soils could indicate that it had been a weed amongst other cereals rather than a crop in its own right, a possibility also proposed by Rösch (1998) (see also the discussion in Behre & Kučan 1994). In the case of the Nydam area with its predominantly clay-rich soils it can not be ascertained if the pollen blew in from more westerly and southern locations or if it was a weed in the area, or alternatively, whether rye was cultivated on a moderate scale during the Iron Age also in Nydam.

The few pollen of *Avena* may have derived either from wild or cultivated oat. According to van Zeist (1974) the earliest finds of certainly cultivated oat species in the Netherlands is Early Medieval, and investigations by Kroll (1987) point to a similar development for the island of Sylt. In other parts of northern Germany *Avena* may have been cultivated from the 1st century BC (Behre 1990). Also Jensen (1985) lists finds of seeds of cultivated oat, *Avena sativa*, from both pre-Roman and Roman Iron age deposits in Denmark, and in the Esbjerg area seeds of oats is know to have been collected during the Iron Age (Robinson 2000). So from a comparison with the above mentioned neighbouring areas it is probable that there was cultivation of oat in addition to other grain species in Iron Age Nydam.

Linum is another species that could have been cultivated close to the bog, at least periodically. Seeds of flax have been found in Iron Age deposits in northern Jutland (Henriksen & Robinson 1996) and the Esbjerg area (Robinson 2000) and it is also known to have been cultivated in the coastal marshes of the Netherlands (van Zeist & Palfenier-Vegter 1991/1992) and was present in NW Germany (Behre & Kučan 1994). The determination in Nydam is not fully ensured, but probable. Its pollen are extremely rare in the pollen diagrams here, a fact that can be attributed to its very poor pollen production and spreading, but possibly also to limited cultivation.

Pollen from *Humulus*, *Cannabis/Humulus* (the pollen from these can not be distinguished in all cases) are represented regularly. It is therefore likely that hop, which can be used to add taste to beer as well as for manufacturing of rope, was known and used in the area.

Apart from the cultivated species mentioned above the pollen in the diagrams most probably include other cultivated plants, but owing to the fact that the pollen can not be determined to species level, such plants do not come out on their own in the diagram. Nevertheless, it is possible that, for example, some of the curves of Apiaceae could include cultivated species of spices and edible vegetables such as caraway, carrot, celery, dill, parsley and parsnip. Likewise the *Sinapis* type pollen contains different plant species, including various cabbages and mustard. Other plants in the same useful and possibly cultivated category might be included in the pollen representation of the Asteraceae and Chenopodiaceae (from which seeds were collected at that time in northern Jutland according to Henriksen & Robinson 1996); probably the green parts of some species of the latter family were used as vegetables. Fabaceae (pea family) are also represented (peas are known to have been cultivated in northern Germany during the Pre-Roman Iron Age according to Behre (1990, see also Rösch 1999), and Celtic beans seem to have been grown in the northeastern Netherlands (van Zeist & Palfenier-Vegter 1991/1992). Also Lactuceae, Lamiaceae and Rosaceae including *Rubus* type (to which raspberry and brambles belong) in the Nydam diagrams could include representation of cultivated and/or used plants. Young leaves of other species, such as *Urtica* and especially rhizones of *Pteridium* could also have added to the food supply (e.g. Göransson 1986). Likewise *Myrica* could have been used. It is known to have been traded in Europe during the Middle Age when it was used together with hop for adding taste and preservation to beer, but seed finds hint that it was also known earlier in Europe (van Zeist 1991) including Denmark (Jensen 1985).

In the diagram there are also various taxa which are today regarded as weeds, but they may at that time have been used for various household purposes. For example *Galium* could have been used with dying of textiles. A great variety, including *Tilia*, *Calluna*, *Hypericum*, *Filipendula* and other Rosaceae, could have served to attract insects, bees in particular, for honey as it is known that honey was collected and used in central Europe at that time (Rösch 1999) and there may have been others of relevance in the kitchen-gardens and fields of a self-supporting society.

Other taxa in the diagram could have had relevance for the livestock. Grass pollen (Poaceae) are plentiful in this part and in spite of the abundant pollen production and good pollen spreading of this family, grasses must have been common in the Nydam area, probably representing both pastures for grazing and meadows for hay making (Behre 1981; Groenman-van Waateringe 1983, 1986) as according to Hodgson et al. (1999) hay making may date back to the Iron Age. The relatively high and fairly constant grass percentages, together with Cyperaceae, *Rumex*, *Plantago lanceolata*, and Ranunculaceae could point to extensive livestock in the area. Besides, *Calluna* may have been used for fodder, in particular for sheep, and there may even have been areas with heather management for grazing as it was the case in western Jutland (Karg 2008). Seeds from oak and beach could have formed a valuable additional food source for swine, and twigs from various trees may have been cut for leaf foddering in winter. *Pteridium* is sometimes also taken as an indicator for grazed forest (Behre 1981).

In addition to the above, most of the trees in the surroundings could have been used. Presence of *Malus/Prunus* type pollen might include representation of apples and prunes. Hazelnuts (*Corylus*) and roasted seeds of beech, *Fagus sylvatica*, are known as dietary objects. Besides, both beech and hazel could provide fire wood. The same goes for oak, *Quercus*, of which the best timber would have been preferred for in- and outdoor construction purposes. Oak needs to reach a fairly high age before the wood is useful with construction purposes, and in order to have long, high quality timber, old, stable, well tended forests are necessary.

Taxus baccata provides excellent wood for bows, and *Salix* (willow) could have been used for numerous purposes ranging from fence constructions and baskets to flutes. A consultation of palaeo-ethnobotanical works (e.g. Brøndegaard 1987) adds many more taxa and now (almost) forgotten uses to the above list.

Apart from the above mentioned plants there are others which point to human activities, for example *Plantago major* (also called the white mans footprints) can indicate frequently trodden places.

From the rather constant and low percentages of charcoal particles of 10 µm long and more, it is suggested that charcoal particles came from heating, cooking and possibly also iron manufacturing, but that there were probably no major forest fires through this time, a conclusion in line with the evidence from the tree pollen curves, which do not indicate major, temporary reductions of trees in the surroundings.

In the upper part of the pre-findlayer part of the section there is presence of *Ruppia* pollen and spines from *Ceratophyllum*. *Ruppia* is an indicator of brackish or marine water, and possibly *Ceratophyllum* indicates the same. These species could have been brought into the locality by fowl or people or be the result of some kind of influence from the sea. If the *Ruppia* pollen was brought in by fowl, for example ducks or geese, it is difficult to explain why they are not represented at deeper levels in the series, because it is very probable that the lake(s) would have been visited by fowl through all the years. It therefore seems more probably that the presence of these species is due either to human transport or are maybe even a result of inundation by brackish water into the area. In the former case the pollen could have been brought in stuck to people or their clothes and equipment. But brackish inundation into the bog area can not be excluded. The marine indicators in the peat deposits in Nydam are situated between 2.3 and 2.45 m above present sea level (see scale in the left hand parts of the pollen diagrams). As late as on 1st November 2006 a high water level reached about 2 m above normal level in the southwestern part of the Baltic Sea (www.dmi.dk/dmi/saadan_steg_vandet_i_baelter_og _sund) and also on previous occasions the water level is known to have been high in the area. For example in 1954,

1941, 1936 and 1935 documented water levels in the areas just north and/or south of Nydam were in the order of almost 2 m higher than the norm, in 1904 it was 2.33 m above and in 1760 it may have been up to 4 m higher than the mean for the area (Gram-Jensen 1991). Further back in time the data become more uncertain, but there is no reason to exclude similarly high water level events during earlier times. For example Gram-Jensen (1991) notes that there were possibly very large floodings in the SW Danish area around 250 AD. Even if these concern the SW coast of Jutland, the possibility of very high water situations and an above normal sea level for a longer period might be supported by investigations by Behre (1986, 2007) and others who have demonstrated that in the North Sea marsh areas the salt water influence reached a relatively high level during the 3d and 4th century AD, a situation that could also have influenced the sea level in the Baltic Sea area.

The values of the added *Lycopodium* spores are fairly constant throughout the pre-findlayer part of the diagram so it may be proposed that the depositional conditions and the pollen influx into the lake during this time were fairly constant.

Overall, the general picture of the environmental conditions during the time until the deposition of the find layer seems to have been one of a stable, well balanced situation probably with a great variety of natural as well as cultivated resources around the bog suggesting rather intensive and prosperous human activity. Seen on the background of the diverse vegetational possibilities and uses, it may be speculated in how far the plants in the lakes were also used. For example, formerly, *Nymphaea* and *Nuphar* were used as medicals; in any case presence of nearby lakes would have contributed to both floral and faunal diversity.

10.2. The time of deposition of the find layer and after

At the time represented by the find layer in series 1, i.e., around 2.60 m, the previously stable picture changed. The same is the case in diagram 2 between 2.28 and 2.32 m at the level of the lower shield. As mentioned in the chapter "Profile Nydam 2, percentage...." it is tempting to suggest that these two horizons are contemporaneous or almost so, because in both diagrams there is a clear decrease in the percentages of pollen from cereals and further there are many parallel trends between curves representing the same pollen types/groups from terrestrial taxa in the two diagrams (accounting for the different sample distances in the two diagrams); i.e., the amount and composition of pollen that blew in from the area around the bog and further away can be expected to be similar in the two diagrams.

At the start of deposition of the find layer in Nydam 1 the concentrations of both tree (AP) and non-tree pollen (NAP) in locality 1 (Fig. 6, 2.60 – 2.62 m) decreased to about a fourth of the previous values, suggesting either that there was a strongly reduced pollen deposition or that the sedimentation rate of other materials had substantially increased, or, possibly a combination of the two.

Further, at the level around the (lower) find layer as reflected by both pollen diagrams (c. 2.6 m in Fig. 4 and c. 2.3 m in Fig. 5) there is a decrease in the pollen percentages from cereals, notably of *Hordeum* and *Triticum;* and hop, *Humulus,* seems to have come to an end. Besides, pollen from *Plantago major* no longer occur. Taken together the changes at this level suggest a change towards decreased human activity and cultivation in the area around Nydam Bog. The tree growth in the surroundings also seems to have been influenced, as it may have become more open as reflected in both the percentage and especially the concentration values.

From the above it may be suggested that the find layer represents a change towards a different and, so it seems, less intensive use of the land, and it is quite possible that there was a collapse of the previous agricultural pattern. The reason for this is not clear and there might be more than one possible explanation:

1) The presence of single brackish/marine pollen a few cm below the find layer might suggest occasional, high sea water levels with intrusion of brackish/marine water that could have influenced the lower lying parts of the valley. Such a situation might have caused a reduction in the extension of pasture areas as expressed in the reduction of pollen from grasses and *Plantago lanceolata* around the time represented by these sediments. Such a possibility might fit in with the slightly higher water level in the German Bay from after 200 AD and on (Behre 1986, 2005).

2) In a locality near Neumünster in northern Germany Garbe-Schönberg et al. (1998) found indications for a steep decline in habitation density after 200 AD. Their record points to field abandonment as reflected both in the mineral tracers and the pollen, the latter of which show a change towards fading evidence of cereal cultivation and low values of other human impact indicators.

3) It could also be speculated that the change in Nydam might be a result of a change in the climatic conditions. From a study of climate change and land-use north and south of the Alps (Tinner et al. 2003) it seems that in a locality in a climatically sensitive area in that part of Europe there was reduced cereal cultivation from 200 AD, a reduction that is proposed to have been a result of a cooler and moister climate. Tinner et al. (2003) suggest that in such a climate the risk of pathogens could have become higher and in turn could have resulted in crop failure. Such a possibility is, however, not supported by an investigation in northern Funen, approximately 75 km north of Nydam, where the vegetational development and the anthropogenic indicators point to a stable situation between 0 and 400 AD. On the background of the results from Funen, it is difficult to envisage that a climate change alone could have caused the changes which took place in the fertile area around the Nydam Bog with its diverse agricultural system, even if there had been a turn towards a cooler and moister climate in Denmark at the time in question.

On the background of the above it might be suggested that agricultural activity represented by this part was strongly reduced as compared to that represented in the pre-findlayer sediments. There is presence of single cereal pollen in the succeeding layers and this could be the result of modest cultivation, but it could equally well represent "naturalized" cereals, although no conclusive evidence can be found for such a hypothesis. Yet, increased percentages of sedges and especially of ferns above the find layer suggest a natural revegetation of the area. This situation remains up to the level at 2.76 m in Profile Nydam 1. From a tentative calculation of the sedimentation rates (see chapter "Age of the series….: Sedimentation rates….") the 10-16 cm of sediment between the (bottom and top of the) find layer in Nydam 1 and the level at 2.76 m may represent a time span in the order of between 20 and 30 years.

At 2.76 m there are clear small maxima in the pollen percentages of various cereal types and Poaceae and there are small maxima of *Galium* as well as of a *Linum* type and charcoal particles at this level. So it seems that for a limited period of time, which probably only spanned a few years, maybe just one or two, there might have been more intensive agricultural use of the area again. From the pollen records it can not be ascertained in how far this level coincides with deposition of artefacts in the lake.

For the succeeding time, represented by the samples at 2.78 m and higher in Nydam 1 and the upper part of Nydam 2, there seems to have been increase in tree growth relative to herbs in the surroundings of the bog. There is presence of single cereal pollen up to 2.91 m as well as of, for example, *Plantago lanceolata*, *Rumex*, *Galium* and *Pteridium* that could point to, but need not indicate, human influence.

Presence of *Typha latifolia*, *Scheuchzeria*, *Menyanthes* and other shallow-water and reed vegetation elements in this part of the diagrams shows that the lake(s) gradually grew over.

From the vegetational development reconstructed from the pollen diagrams it seems that the events which took place at the time of the lower find layer in Nydam 1 had long term consequences for the way of living in the area. Even if there are indications for an attempt to return to the "traditional" farming at 2.76 m in Nydam 1, and also maybe modestly so for the time represented from this level and up to 2.91 m, the more intensive and diverse pre-findlayer farming and pasture system does not seem to have become re-established.

The uppermost part of Nydam 1 (from 3.00 m and up) has a high content of undeterminable (corroded) pollen as it is also the case in the upper part of Nydam 2, so it seems that the upper sediments in the bog have been exposed to oxygen and besides, sediments of different age have possibly become mixed by trampling. Therefore no conclusions are made for this part.

11. Conclusions

The two pollen diagrams from Nydam Bog show the vegetational development and human influence during the younger part of the Iron Age in the area. The development represented by the diagrams overlap in time with archaeological finds of boats, weapons and other artefacts. During the whole period represented by the investigated records, there seems to have been a diversity of trees in the surroundings, but the forest density has probably been moderate. For the time until the deposition of the lower archaeological find layer, the pollen composition points to a stable, self-sustaining community with a variety of natural resources, and relatively large areas may have been occupied by arable land and pastures. Around the time of the deposition of the artefacts and during the succeeding time peoples' use of the landscape seems to have changed, and according to the pollen diagrams only one short, relatively intensive cultivation phase took place after deposition of the first archaeological layer.

The development of the lake could have been a rather sudden event that started after Iron Age human agricultural activity was well established in the area. The development of a lake with open water and a reed zone could have made the already rich area even more attractive, because new additional resources like fish, fowl and water/reed vegetation might have been added to the cultivated/domesticated and natural terrestrial resources.

A comparison between the two pollen records shows that they agree in principle on the composition and development of pollen from terrestrial plants, but differ with regard to the successional development of the water plants. This difference may be related to their different proximity to archaeological finds because in Nydam 2 human activity may have caused vertical mixing of the sediments. On the other hand the location of the pollen diagrams near archaeological finds has the advantage that it can offer a direct relationship between archaeological events and vegetational and environmental changes within the area.

12. Acknowledgements

I am grateful to Charlie Christensen, the National Museum of Denmark, for help with the profile descriptions in the field and the sampling for radiocarbon dating. Nationalmuseet carried out the radiocarbon datings. The National Research Council of Humanities supported the investigations through grant numbers 15-8009-1 JEK and 15-8681-1 JLU/gj. Tage Thyrsted gave helpful comments to the manuscript and Leif Aas Andersen, Sønderborg, helped with information on high water levels during the past centuries. Nydamselskabet kindly kept me informed about the progress with the work in the bog. The skilful help with the figures by Lars Foged Thomsen, Moesgård Museum is much appreciated as is the continuous support and constructive comments of Jørgen Ilkjær, also Moesgård Museum.

13. References

Andersen, A. 1954, Two standard pollen diagrams from south Jutland. *Danmarks Geologiske Undersøgelse* II, 80, 188-209.

Andreasen, E.R. & Christensen, C. 1998, Pollenanalytisk undersøgelse af brednært profil i Nydam Mose. *Nationalmusets Naturvidenskabelige undersøgelser Rapport* 43, 1-22.

Behre, K.-E. 1981, The interpretation of anthropogenic indicators in pollen diagrams. *Pollen et Spores* 23, 2, 225-245.

Behre, K.-E. 1986, Meeresspiegelverhalten und Besiedlung während der Zeit um Christi Geburt in den Nordseemarschen, *Offa* 43, 45-53.

Behre, K.-E. 1990, Kulturpflanzen und Unkräuter der vorrömischen Eisenzeit aus der Siedlund Rullstorf, Ldkr. Lüneburg. *Nachrichten aus Niedersachsens Urgeschichte* 59, 141-165.

Behre, K.-E. 1992, The history of rye cultivation in Europe. *Vegetation History and Archaeobotany* 1, 141-156.

Behre, K.-E. 2005, Meeresspiegelanstieg – Marschentwicklund – Küstenlinien. Die letzten 10 000 Jahre an der deutschen Nordseeküste im Zeitraffer. *Schriftenreihe des Landesmuseums Natur und Mensch, Oldenburg* 33, 25-36.

Behre, K.-E. 2007, A new Holocene sea-level curve for the southern North Sea. *Boreas* 36: 82-102.

Behre, K.-E. & Kučan, D. 1994, Die Geschichte der Kulturlandschaft und des Ackerbaus in der Siedlungskammer Flögeln, Niedersachsen, seit der Jungsteinzeit. *Probleme der Küstenforschung im südlichen Nordseegebiet* 21. Isensee Oldenburg.

Bonde, N. & Daly, A. 2000, Dendrokronologisk undersøgelse af "den sønderhuggede egebåd" fra Nydam Mose Sønderjyllands amt. *Nationalmuseets Naturvidenskabelige Undersøgelser Rapport* 3, 1-13.

Brøndegaard, V.J. 1987, *Folk og flora*, 1-4. Rosenkilde og Bagger, Danmark.

Christensen, C. & Kolstrup, E. 1998, Nydam Mose – en jernaldersø med krigsbytteofre. *GeologiskNyt* 6, 6-9.

Dörfler, W. 1989, Pollenanalytische Untersuchungen zur Vegetations- und Siedlungsgeschichte im Süden des Landkreises Cuxhaven, Niedersachsen. *Probleme der Küstenforschung im südlichen Nordseegebiet* 17, 1-75.

Fægri, K. & Iversen, J. 1966, *Textbook of pollen analysis*. Munksgaard, Copenhagen

Gaillard, M.-J. 1984, A palaeohydrological study of Krageholmssjön (Scania, south Sweden). *Lundqua report* 25, 40 pp.

Garbe-Schönberg, C.-D., Wiethold, J., Butenhoff, D., Utech, C. & Stoffers, P. 1998, Geochemical and palynological record in annually laminated sediments from Lake Belau (Schleswig-Holstein) reflecting paleoecology and human impact over 9000 a. *Meyniana* 50, 47-70.

Gram-Jensen, I. 1991, Stormfloder. *Danish Meteorological Institute, Scientific Report* 91-1: 1-121. DMI Copenhagen

Groenman-van Waateringe, W. 1983, The early agricultural utilization of the Irish landscape: The last word on the elm decline? *BAR British Series* 116, 217-232.

Groenman-van Waateringe 1986, Grazing possibilities in the Neolithic of the Netherlands based on palynological data. In: K.-E. Behre (Ed.) *Anthropogenic indicators in pollen diagrams*. Balkema, Rotterdam 187-202.

Göransson, H. 1986, Man and the Forests of Nemoral Broad-Leafed Trees During the Stone Age. *Striae* 24, 143-152.

Henriksen, P.S. 2003, Rye cultivation in the Danish Iron Age – some new evidence from iron-smelting furnaces. *Vegetation History and Archaeobotany* 12, 177-185.

Henriksen, P.S. & Robinson, D. 1996, Early Iron Age agriculture: archaeobotanial evidence from an underground granary at Overbygård in northern Jutland, Denmark. *Vegetation History and Archaeobotany* 5, 1-11.

Hodgson, J.G., Halstead, P., Wilson, P.J. & Davis, S. 1999, Functional interpretation of archaeobotanical data: making hay in the archaeological record. *Vegetation History and Archaeobotany* 8, 261-271.

Jensen, H.A. 1985, Catalogue of late- and post-glacial macrofossils of Spermatophyta from Denmark, Schleswig, Scania, Halland and Blekinge dated 13,000 B.P. to 1536 A.D. *Danmarks Geologiske Undersøgelse*, A, 6, 1-91.

Jessen, A. 1945, Beskrivelse til Geologisk Kort over Danmark 1:100.000. Kortbladet Sønderborg. *Danmarks Geologiske Undersøgelse*, I, 20, 91pp.

Jørgensen, M.E., Møller, H.-M.F. & Pedersen, K.J. 1998, GIS og Nydam Mose – GIS anvendt som analyseværktøj. *GeologiskNyt* 6, 11-13.

Karg, S. 2008, Direct evidence of heathland management in the early Bronze Age (14th century B.C.) from the grave-mound Skelhøj in western Denmark. *Vegetation History and Archaeobotany* 17, 41-49.

Kolstrup, E. 2005, A pollen preparation procedure with soap wash-sieving for fine-grained unconsolidated sediments. *Kvinner i arkeologi i Norge* 25, 50-59.

Kroll, H.J. 1987, Vor- und frühgeschichtlicher Ackerbau in Archsum auf Sylt. Eine botanische Grossrestanalyse. In: Kossack, G., Averdieck, R.-R., Blume, H.-P., Harck, O., Hoffmann, D. (Eds) Archsum auf Sylt Teil 2, Landwirtschaft und Umwelt in vor- und frühgeschichtlicher Zeit. Studien zur Küstenarchäologie Schleswig-Holsteins, Ser. B, Bd 2. *Römisch-Germanische Forschungen* 44, 51-158.

Mikkelsen, V.M. 1949, Præstø Fjord. The development of the Post-Glacial vegetation and a contribution to the history of the Baltic Sea. *Dansk Botanisk Arkiv*, 13, 5, 171pp.

Moore, P.E., Webb, J.A. & Collinson, M.E. 1991, *Pollen analysis*, 2nd Ed. Blackwell Scientific, Oxford.

Nilsson, T. 1935 Die pollenanalytische Zonengliederung der spät- und postglazialen Bildungen Schonens. *Meddelanden från Lunds Geologisk-Mineralogiska Institution* 61, 385-562.

Nilsson, T. 1964, Standardpollendiagramme und C-14 Datierungen aus dem Ageröds Mosse im mittleren Schonen. *Lunds Universitäts Årsskrift*, N.F. 2, 59, 7, 52pp.

Odgaard, B.V. 1994, The Holocene vegetation history of northern West Jutland, Denmark. *Opera Botanica* 123, 1-171.

Olsson, I.U. 1985, I. Radiocarbon Dating. In: B.E. Berglund (Ed.) *Handbook of Holocene Palaeoecology and Palaeohydrology*. Wiley, Chichester. 275-312.

Punt, W. (Ed.) 1976, *The Northwest European Pollen Flora* 1, Elsevier, Amsterdam.

Punt, W. & Blackmore, S (Eds) 1984, *The Northwest European Pollen Flora* 6, Elsevier, Amsterdam.

Punt, W. & Clarke, G.C.S. (Eds) 1980, *The Northwest European Pollen Flora* 2, Elsevier, Amsterdam.

Punt, W. & Clarke, G.C.S. (Eds) 1981, *The Northwest European Pollen Flora* 3, Elsevier, Amsterdam.

Punt, W. & Clarke, G.C.S. (Eds) 1984, *The Northwest European Pollen Flora* 4, Elsevier, Amsterdam.

Punt, W., Blackmore, S. & Clarke, G.C.S. (Eds) 1988, *The Northwest European Pollen Flora* 5, Elsevier, Amsterdam.

Rasmussen, P. 2005, Mid- to late-Holocene land-use change and lake development at Dallund Sø, Denmark: vegetation and land-use history inferred from pollen data. *The Holocene* 15, 8, 1116-1129.

Rieck, F., Jørgensen, E., Petersen, P.V. & Christensen, C. 1999, "... som samlede Ofre fra en talrig Krigerflok". Status over Nationalmuseets Nydamprojekt 1989-1997. *Nationalmuseets Arbejdsmark* 1999, 10-34.

Robinson, D. 2000, Charred plant remains in two pottery vessels from the Early Roman Iron Age at Præstestien. In Siemen, P. (Ed.) Præstestien, Settlement from 4th – 9th Century vol 1. *Arkæologiske Rapporter 3, Esbjerg Museum*, 143-151.

Rösch, M. 1998, The history of crops and crop weeds in south-western Germany from the Neolithic period to modern times, as shown by archaeobotanical evidence. *Vegetation History and Archaeobotany* 7, 109-125.

Rösch, M. 1999, Evaluation of honey residues from Iron Age hill-top sites in south-western Germarny: implications for local and regional land use and vegetation dynamics. *Vegetation History and Archaeobotany* 8, 105-112.

Stuiver, M., Reimer, P. J., Bard, E., Beck, J. W., Burr, G. S., Hughen, K. A., Kromer, B., Mccormac, G., van der Plicht, J. & Spurk, M. 1998, INTCAL98 radiocarbon age calibration, 24.000-0 cal bp. *Radiocarbon* 40(3), 1041-1083.

Tinner, W., Lotter, A.F., Ammann, B., Conedera, M., Hubschmid, P., van Leeuwen, J.F.N. & Wehrli, M. 2003, Climate change and contemporaneous land-use phases north and south of the Alps 2300 BC to 800 AD. *Quaternary Science Reviews* 22, 1447-1460.

Stockmarr, J. 1971, Tablets with spores used in absolute pollen analysis. *Pollen et Spores* 13, 615-621.

van Zeist, W. 1974, Palaeobotanical studies of settlement sites in the coastal area of the Netherlands. *Palaeohistoria* 16, 223-371.

van Zeist, W. 1991, Economic aspects. In: van Zeist, W., Wasylikowa, K & Behre, K.-E. (Eds) *Progress in Old World Palaeoethnobotany*. Balkema, Rotterdam, 109-129.

van Zeist, W. & Palfenier-Vegter, R.M. 1991/1992 Roman Iron Age plant husbandry at Peelo, the Netherlands. *Palaeohistoria* 33/34, 287-297.

Wiethold, J. 1998, Studien zur jüngeren postglazialen Vegetations- und Siedlungsgeschichte im östlichen Schleswig-Holstein. *Universitätsforschungen zur prähistorischen Archäologie. Aus dem Institut für Ur- und Frühgeschichte der Universität Kiel Bd. 45*. Rudolf Habelt, Bonn.

www.dmi.dk/dmi/saadan_steg_vandet_i_baelter_og_sund (1st Dec. 2008).

Appendix 1A

List of some names in the pollen diagrams according to their appearance in the diagram. Not all names are included, and where more types are included a common name is chosen.

LATIN NAME	ENGLISH NAME	DANISH NAME
Pinus	Pine	Fyr
Picea	Spruce	Gran
Betula	Birch	Birk
Salix	Willow	Pil
Alnus	Alder	El
Corylus	Hazel	Hassel
Quercus	Oak	Eg
Ulmus	Elm	Ælm
Tilia	Lime	Lind
Fraxinus	Ash	Ask
Rhamnus catharticus	Buckthorn	Vrietorn
Rhamnus frangula	Alder buckthorn	Tørstetræ
Acer	Maple	Løn
Fagus	Beech	Bøg
Carpinus	Hornbeam	Avnbøg
Taxus	Yew	Taks
Populus	Poplar	Poppel
Crataegus	Hawthorn	Tjørn
Malus	Apple	Æble
Prunus	Cherry	Blomme, Kirsebær
Sorbus	Rowan	Røn
Sambucus	Elder	Hyld
Viburnum	Guelder rose	Kvalkved
Myrica	Bog myrtle	Pors
Hedera	Ivy	Vedbend
Apiaceae	Parsley family	Skærmplantefamilien
Asteraceae	Aster family	Kurvblomstfamilien
Artemisia	Mugwort	Bynke
Brassicaceae	Mustard family	Korsblomstfamilien
Sinapis	Mustard	Sennep
Humulus	Hop	Humle
Caryophyllaceae	Pink family	Nellikefamilien
Chenopodiaceae	Goosefoot family	Salturtfamilien
Cyperaceae	Sedges	Halvgræsser
Empetrum	Crowberry	Revling

Calluna	Heather	Lyng
Fabaceae	Legumes	Ærteblomstfamilien
Juncaceae	Rush family	Sivfamilien
Lactuceae	Lettuce	Salat
Linum	Flax	Hør
Plantago lanceolata	Ribwort plantain	Lancet vejbred
Plantago major	Greater plantain	Glat vejbred
Avena	Oat	Havre
Cereal	Cereals	Korn generelt
Hordeum	Barley	Byg
Secale	Rye	Rug
Triticum	Wheat	Hvede
Poaceae	Grass family	Græsser
Rumex	Dock	Skræppe
Caltha	Kingcup	Kabbeleje
Ranunculus	Buttercup	Ranunkel
Filipendula	Meadowsweet	Mjødurt
Potentilla	Cinquefoil	Potentil
Rubus	Blackberry	Hindbær, Brombær
Galium	Bedstraw	Snerre
Urtica	Nettle	Nælde
Dryopteris felix-mas		Mangeløv
Pteridium	Bracken	Ørnebregne
Filicales		Bregner
Scheuchzeria	Rannoch rush	Blomstersiv
Lemna	Duckweed	Andemad
Menyanthes	Buckbean	Bukkeblad
Nuphar	Yellow water-lily	Gul åkande
Nymphaea	White water-lily	Hvid åkande
Potamogeton	Pondweed	Vandaks
Ruppia	Tasselweed	Havgræs
Sparganium	Bur-reed	Pindsvineknop
Typha latifolia	Reedmace	Bredbladet dunhammer
Ceratophyllum	Horn-wort	Hornblad

Appendix 1B

List of some names in the pollen diagrams in alphabetic order. Not all names are included, and where more types are included a common name is chosen.

LATIN NAME	ENGLISH NAME	DANISH NAME
Acer	Maple	Løn
Alnus	Alder	El
Apiaceae	Parsley family	Skærmplantefamilien
Artemisia	Mugwort	Bynke
Asteraceae	Aster family	Kurvblomstfamilien
Avena	Oat	Havre
Betula	Birch	Birk
Brassicaceae	Mustard family	Korsblomstfamilien
Carpinus	Hornbeam	Avnbøg
Calluna	Heather	Lyng
Caltha	Kingcup	Kabbeleje
Caryophyllaceae	Pink family	Nellikefamilien
Ceratophyllum	Horn-wort	Hornblad
Cereal	Cereals	Korn generelt
Chenopodiaceae	Goosefoot family	Salturtfamilien
Corylus	Hazel	Hassel
Crataegus	Hawthorn	Tjørn
Cyperaceae	Sedges	Halvgræsser
Dryopteris felix-mas		Mangeløv
Empetrum	Crowberry	Revling
Fabaceae	Legumes	Ærteblomstfamilien
Fagus	Beech	Bøg
Filicales		Bregner
Filipendula	Meadowsweet	Mjødurt
Fraxinus	Ash	Ask
Galium	Bedstraw	Snerre
Hedera	Ivy	Vedbend
Hordeum	Barley	Byg
Humulus	Hop	Humle
Juncaceae	Rush family	Sivfamilien
Lactuceae	Lettuce	Salat
Lemna	Duckweed	Andemad
Linum	Flax	Hør
Malus	Apple	Æble
Menyanthes	Buckbean	Bukkeblad

Myrica	Bog myrtle	Pors
Nuphar	Yellow water-lily	Gul åkande
Nymphaea	White water-lily	Hvid åkande
Picea	Spruce	Gran
Pinus	Pine	Fyr
Plantago lanceolata	Ribwort plantain	Lancet vejbred
Plantago major	Greater plantain	Glat vejbred
Poaceae	Grass family	Græsser
Populus	Poplar	Poppel
Potamogeton	Pondweed	Vandaks
Potentilla	Cinquefoil	Potentil
Prunus	Cherry	Blomme, Kirsebær
Pteridium	Bracken	Ørnebregne
Quercus	Oak	Eg
Ranunculus	Buttercup	Ranunkel
Rhamnus catharticus	Buckthorn	Vrietorn
Rhamnus frangula	Alder buckthorn	Tørstetræ
Rubus	Blackberry	Hindbær, Brombær
Rumex	Dock	Skræppe
Ruppia	Tasselweed	Havgræs
Salix	Willow	Pil
Sambucus	Elder	Hyld
Scheuchzeria	Rannoch rush	Blomstersiv
Secale	Rye	Rug
Sinapis	Mustard	Sennep
Sorbus	Rowan	Røn
Sparganium	Bur-reed	Pindsvineknop
Taxus	Yew	Taks
Tilia	Lime	Lind
Triticum	Wheat	Hvede
Typha latifolia	Reedmace	Bredbladet dunhammer
Ulmus	Elm	Ælm
Urtica	Nettle	Nælde
Viburnum	Guelder rose	Kvalkved